TAO
OF
MUSIC

TAO OF MUSIC
Experiencing Life As Music

Bodhi Setchko

Crystal Wind Publishing
P.O. Box 150724
San Rafael, CA 94915

TAO OF MUSIC
Experiencing Life As Music

Crystal Wind Publishing
P.O. Box 150724
San Rafael, CA 94915
415-485-1327
bodhisetchko.com
ksetchko@yahoo.com

1st Printing Spring 2016
ISBN: 978-0-9973404-0-2

Author: Bodhi Setchko
Cover (and interior) design: Bodhi Setchko
Graphics layout: Brad Reynolds integralartandstudies.com
Cover Art: Music Bird: Public Domain
Inside Art: Bodhi Setchko
Photos of Bodhi: Deborah Welsh deborahwelsh.com

*This book is dedicated
to the loving memory of my parents,
Edward and Penelope Setchko*

CONTENTS

AWAKENING TO THE PATH

ON THE PATH

CHALLENGES ON THE PATH

ONE WITH THE PATH

LETTING GO OF THE PATH

EPILOGUE

INSPIRATIONAL RESOURCES

OTHER WORKS BY BODHI

ABOUT BODHI

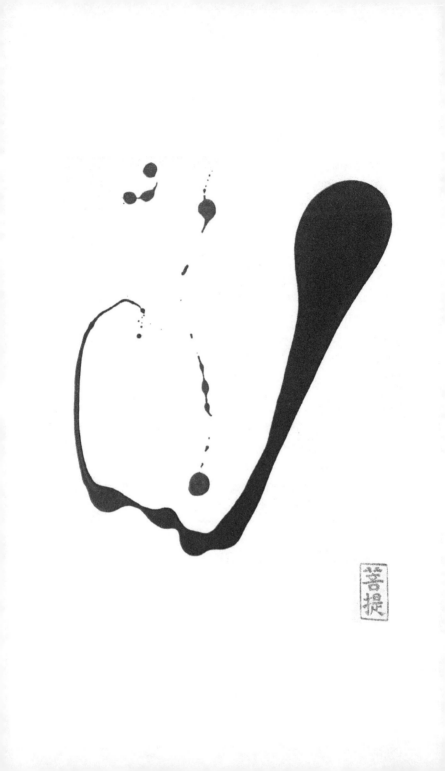

Foreword

Sometimes a single stone lying at the tides' edge, glistening among hundreds of other polished stones, calls to you. That color, that particular shape, seems so much a part of the fresh and carefree moment that you bend to pick it up. You hold it close in your hand, as you now hold this book. Somehow it mirrors your joy and, almost without thinking, you put it in your pocket as a reminder of the simple gift that a walk on the beach can be.

Each of these short meditations on life as music shine with that elegant simplicity. They are meant to invoke a quiet attention to the wonder of sound. They point to, as well as come from, a lifetime of musical discovery. Yet unlike that bright pebble, its color doesn't fade over time. Somehow it keeps glistening with the symphony of the surf that washed over it.

Bodhi invites us to listen to our lives with a relaxed attentiveness, opening us to the radiant possibilities of rhythm and silent interval that each breath holds. These are gifts from a man who has lived his life combing the musical beaches of our world. And what follows are the fine stones he has found. He offers us a way, a Tao, of keeping the sheen of sonic exploration alive, moment by moment. Who knows? You might awaken a new melody in the song of your life.

Patrick Woodworth
Poet and Radio Host
From the River's Mouth

An Invitation

Without music, life would be a mistake.

— *Frederich Nietzsche*

This book is an invitation to enter into the journey of your own creativity. It is the beginning of a trail that invites you to walk its path. Each being on this planet Earth discovers their own way of living. Just to be alive is a very complex, creative process. Yet, paradoxically, things can appear to be quite simple at times. There are consistent patterns we can see, learn from, and tune into. These rhythmic cycles are a guide to being in the flow, the watercourse way of grace and ease.

Music and sound are natural tools for the joyful expression of this awareness. We repeat songs as a way of anchoring our body in the natural groove of life. We drum to celebrate our heartbeat. Our breath is free like the wind and the dance of life uninhibited.

The Tao of Music unfolds one step at a time. Everyone travels at their own pace and everything is connected. When we are free to explore our own creativity, miracles happen. Each of the chapters in this book is a seed poem that you can plant in the soil of your consciousness. Explore the *Awareness Practices* to water the seedlings and notice how they blossom. You might be pleasantly surprised by the harvest.

Let us begin by reflecting upon these words...

Origin of TAO
Chinese *Dào*, literally means *Way*

Definitions of TAO
- The unconditional unknowable source and guiding principle of all reality.

- The process of nature by which all things change and which is to be followed for a life of harmony.

- The art or skill of doing something in harmony with the essential nature of the thing.

Origins of MUSIC
Middle English *Musik*, Anglo-French *Musike*, Latin *Musica*, Greek *Mousikē*, *Mousikos* of the Muses

Definitions of MUSIC
- Vocal, instrumental, or mechanical sounds having rhythm, melody, or harmony.

- Sounds that are sung by voices or played on musical instruments.

- The science and art of ordering tones or sounds in succession, in combination, and in temporal relationships to produce a composition having unity and continuity.

AWAKENING
TO THE PATH

Tao Is Infinitely Varied

Can you hear it? The music. I can hear it everywhere.
In the wind, in the air, in the light. It's all around us.
All you have to do is open yourself up.
All you have to do is listen.

— *August Rush*

Listening to the rhythmic patterns of raindrops on the roof as I wake in the morning, I realize that nature is infinitely creative in the ways it expresses itself. And it's all musical. As a human being, I tend to imagine my creative expression is only heard and experienced by other human beings. Yet as I listen, learn and derive pleasure and nurturance from the wind, rain, and the songs of animals and birds, perhaps all of nature is listening to me as well.

When I was young, I had a very unusual experience while camping in Jasper National Park in Canada. I was playing my flute in a meadow on a pleasant Spring afternoon. All of a sudden, a bear appeared out of the forest. At first I was quite surprised and felt my heartbeat go into double-time. Then I remembered that it's a common practice to make some noise to scare the bear away. So I started playing faster and louder, trying to imitate some pots and pans clanging. I think I may have even improvised a fast, high pitched Latin music solo. Or maybe it was just confused noise. I don't remember what I played. It felt like a long time but was probably only a few minutes.

Then I realized that during this whole time the bear was listening to me. He stood there, peacefully taking in the strange, nervous human in front of him. I was relieved when he turned and went on his way. I sat down to calm myself, trusting I was OK. I suppose if I were a Buddha, and not afraid of death, I would have been more relaxed. I'd have just smiled and played a simple melody for my furry friend. I think we both were amused by this chance encounter in the Canadian wilderness.

The Way is unique to each living being. Plants, animals and humans alike all have preferences. These proclivities of desire sprout from within as petals from a flower seed. Every individual finds sustenance in their own way. Some thrive on the resonance of loud dance beats, others on the rich texture of a symphony orchestra or the quiet ripples of a stream as the water flows over the rocks.

In the world of music, the myriad styles and forms all arise out of the uniqueness of the environment in which they are born. Sound is an expression of the reality that surrounds us. It's all music and inspires us each in unique ways. The music we create must surely reflect our experience.

I have heard that prayer is mostly about paying attention and being fully present to the moment at hand. Tao is also about presence. Whether we create sounds on an instrument, chant with our voice or simply follow our breath, there is a magical power in tuning into our own rhythms. Every living thing has a distinct life design. This practice of presence allows us to recognize and harmonize with our unique, inner patterns.

As each individual realizes and awakens to their own music, the whole universe aligns itself in perfect balance. There is unity within the diversity. The world unfolds as a dynamic and dramatic interspecies musical.

Awareness Practice

The next time you find yourself in the midst of a thunderstorm, in a stadium full of people, in a forest of tall trees or next to the freeway, stop and listen. See how many different sounds you can discern. Notice the tempo and dynamics. Feel it breathing in rhythmic waves of expression. Notice if you feel nurtured or not by this intimate connection. You can learn a lot about the type of environments that best suit you by paying attention in this way. Whatever your experience, it's right for you. Tao is infinitely varied.

Rhythm Of Life

If a man does not keep pace with his companions,
perhaps it is because he hears a different drummer.
Let him step to the music which he hears,
however measured or far away.

— *Henry David Thoreau*

Ah 1...2... Ah 1 2 3 4... It all starts with rhythm, the beat and time. Most of us want to be in the band, be on the team, be a part of something and find our groove in life. It's a wonderful thing to meet kindred souls on the journey. How magical it is, jamming with friends to create harmony and beauty and have fun!

And yet, sometimes we dance alone. It's good to learn how to be comfortable in our own skin. In order to be ourselves fully in the ensemble, we have to develop our talent and learn to love ourselves. This inner-outer, back and forth reality manifests in each of us as a unique pattern.

It took me years to be at ease in my own body. I was very active as a child. It's possible I would have been diagnosed with ADHD. Thank God it was before the days of automatic drug prescriptions. I was a kinetic learner, wanting to experience everything directly. Although I read a lot of books, I was not much into studying. Practicing musical instruments was my favorite activity. The accordion, trumpet and piano occupied my time until I was fifteen. The flute then entered my world and has stayed with me ever since.

My love of nature kept me hiking and biking in the hills at the edge of the town where I grew up. I walked a couple of miles to school every day and was very involved in sports. Relaxing was not my specialty! At sixteen I learned to practice yoga. The alternating effect of effort and calm started to reset my natural energy flow. I believe this was my saving grace and set me on the road to equanimity.

It's been said that to be happy, know thyself. I would expand on that and venture that another facet of happiness and joy is knowing how to blend with other creative people, musicians and artists of every discipline. Discovering when to play and when not to play. Knowing when to speak and when to refrain. Intuiting when to move and when to be still. Should we add some color, or stand back and observe? How do we gracefully weave who we are into the greater symphony that surrounds us?

This cycle of solitude and society, tempering our own gifts and skills to play in the orchestra, is one of the greatest balancing acts we can learn to master.

Awareness Practice

As you go about your life, notice what you are drawn to, what invites your participation. When you first become aware of something intriguing, stop, look and listen. Pay attention without any expectations. Just be curious and open. You might be thinking about how cool it is or there might be a bodily sensation arising in your bones, almost a spiritual revelation. Whatever you are feeling, it's the beginning of a relationship. If there is truly a genuine resonance with your soul, there will be many opportunities to get to know more about it and develop a deeper connection over time. Relax into the art form and let it reveal its essence to you.

Entering The Conversation

Tao, the oldest philosophy of life,
gives a simple answer: Life is living, and our task
is to live wholesomely, happily and freely.

— Jolan Chang

This is my first book. Sometimes I feel like a little child on the sidelines, wanting to be part of the scene, to join the fun and be heard. I want to participate in the dance of words. I ask myself, "Will I have something meaningful to say? Can I add to the story? Will others want to listen?"

These questions float through my consciousness as I develop a new skill set. Perhaps you have similar thoughts when you expand into new creative territory. It's a whole new ballgame, organizing my thoughts in chapters instead of chords, melodies and time signatures. Though the rhythm and flow of book writing is different, the discipline is a variation of my past experience in practicing scales and composing music.

My literary friends tell me that writing a book is about entering a conversation, one that is ongoing and has been since language began. First we listen, and then we join the chorus. It's about the exchange of ideas and finding our tribe. I seek to connect with those who have a similar desire to *jam* on topics that are mutually stimulating.

As I embark upon this journey, I embrace an

attitude of beginner's mind. After years of teaching and performing music, I am once again a novice. Essentially, it's a spiritual pilgrimage and the world of words is opening up to me. The music of words is singing through me. I remember the old saying, *Success is all about showing up.* So I sit down, breathe, and open my heart-mind to receive guidance. I trust the destination will make itself known.

I am writing for music lovers, listeners, professionals, hobbyists and anyone who is intrigued by the world of sound. I hope to offer insights into the journey and perhaps inspire a deeper exploration into the mystery that music is.

All of the myriad art forms created by humans have an internal and external component. We do the inner work in order to have the tools and skills for outer expression. Entering the field of play and smoothly exiting is an art form in itself. Being present is the most important thing. When we recognize this, the pressure to be brilliant or anything else other than our natural, divine self, is eliminated. The need to impress others is removed from the space. How refreshing it is, allowing the words to flow, and then pausing to hear them land. Let us listen with full attention to one another, relaxing into the creative milieu with our whole being.

Just as in music, the spaces in-between the words are also part of the interaction. A silent smile can convey a deep understanding or an appreciation of an idea. The conversation reflects the terrain of the environment we inhabit together. Each voice offers itself as part of the tapestry and the bigger picture unfolds in harmony.

Awareness Practice

Repeating positive affirmations is a great way to manifest the changes that you desire in your life. This practice can be especially helpful when you are starting out on a new path. The following exercise can assist you to create your own.

Get comfortable, set a timer for 7-10 minutes, and just write. List everything you want as if it's real now, in this moment. Keep the pen moving without leaving the paper and don't edit. Just keep going until the timer chimes. When you are finished, go back over the writing and circle the words that speak to you most clearly and inspire you. Write all of these words or phrases on a separate piece of paper. Play with the order and weave them into your own personal affirmation. Remember to keep it in the present tense. If you're with a group, you may want to share what you've written. Hearing it out loud can amplify its power.

Find a rhythm for it and repeat it a few times. If you can add a little melody it will become a *songfirmation*, an affirmation in song. You might find it useful in keeping on track with your purpose and vision.

Liquid Music

What you hear is real to you,
but only on the particular level
to which you've developed your aural sense.
You can expand your reality
by learning new ways of listening.

— *Bodhi Setchko*

I was immersed in a strange world of sound, such as I had never experienced before. There was a tingling sensation throughout my body and I seemed to melt into each particular sound as it was created. The wind floated through my consciousness and I *saw* the glimmer of leaves but *felt* the rustling inside my head. The whole process of perception seemed to be reversed. I knew exactly what was happening before it did. As I became more aware of this, it appeared that I was encapsulated in a time vacuum where everything was happening simultaneously and I was able to experience it as such.

As I concentrated my gaze toward the mountains of the north, the sounds became prominent again. I realized how I had tuned them out as my mind tried to understand and describe what was happening in the world around me. All of these elements had a subtle way of coaxing me to concentrate and I knew I should focus all my attention on *hearing*.

Then the wind slipped through the bushes again,

and the prickly sound tickled a chord inside that made me think I had a place in this beautiful orchestra. There were holes within the emerging patterns. The clouds punctuated these spaces with an airy, gong-like expansiveness. Each separate, distinct sound ricocheted off my eardrums.

I looked down into my hands at the simple, one-stringed instrument that I had crafted, my *Spirit Catcher*. I raised it up, plucked the string and joined in the symphony, merging completely with this wonderful world of liquid music.

Awareness Practice

Do you remember your daydreams, your dreams or visions? The next time you are relaxing or meditating, feel the expansive quality of your *seeing*, *feeling*, and *hearing*. How do your senses interact? Maybe this heightened awareness allows you to see and feel with greater depth and perceive sounds from a much further distance than you had imagined you could. Perhaps you can place them in a stereo, quadrophonic or surround-sound field of awareness. Can you hear in your inner ear the soft and subtle ringing tones of your own body? How much richer and textured does your environment seem now? Does this practice stimulate your creativity?

ON THE PATH

Why Practice?

Don't ask, practice.
Some questions no one can answer but yourself.
Practice and the answers will come to you in time.
The only route to understanding 'The Way' is
through your own experience.

— *Philip Toshio Sudo*

It's uncanny how some people can practice and practice, work hard, and still never achieve success. It may appear that another person just gets it easily. There seems to be some sort of luck involved. But is there? Any kind of practice is basically repetition, going over something again and again. Composer and pianist W. A. Mathieu says, *Music practice lights up the inner life.*

Some say you will gain mastery by doing anything for 10,000 hours. After feeling comfortable and at ease with some creative expression, sharing it with the world is a natural extension of your practice. I think if you get really good at something, maybe even famous, you better enjoy it. You may have to perform it 10,000 times or more!

Maybe you love nursery rhymes. You know dozens of them and have perhaps even written a few. One day you're humming a simple tune in the park and a professional agent hears you, and wants to record your melodies. The music catches on and you find yourself singing and teaching nursery rhymes all over the world. This path or Tao of Nursery Rhymes, evolved simply from doing something that you love, over and over. You never tire of it. It's your natural way.

There were two periods of my life that were all about practicing music. I wanted to learn the ins and outs of all 12 keys. First on the flute and then later on the piano. There was a natural rhythm that evolved from my intention to get through as many permutations of every scale over the time frame of a week. As I made my way through the keys, so many melodies revealed themselves to me. To this day I remember that phase of my training and appreciate the ability it gave me to be musically flexible when performing with other musicians.

Find what you love to do and keep doing it. Do it from love and your Way, your Tao of Music will be revealed. This is why we practice for self-fulfillment first and performance second. Practicing for the love of your craft brings great joy. And your joy will naturally enhance your performance and be sensed by those who experience your work.

Awareness Practice

Some say *Practice makes perfect*. Others say you're perfect just the way you are. A Taoist approach might be, *Practice IS the way*. Whenever we are learning something new, there is always a period of repetition, going over and over the simplest thing until it becomes second nature. The secret is to love the process. By enjoying each small step up the mountain, practice becomes joyful instead of a task or a burden.

Eventually we understand that *Life is practice*. We've been practicing from the instant we were born. It's just the subject that keeps changing as we learn new things. After you have practiced something a thousand times, remember this present moment. THIS moment is the Tao. Recognize it and whatever you aspire to learn is just one step in front of you.

Body Rhythms

Music is sound. Sound is vibration.
Vibration is life. Life is music.

— Bodhi Setchko

Life is vibration. Energy waves are moving through time and space. Color waves are perceived by the eyes and sound waves by the ears. We also *feel* the waves, like the sensation of sound coming through a bass sub-woofer shaking our bones. The more we attune ourselves to different frequencies in our world, the more sensitive we become to the environment we inhabit. We recognize that we are an intricate part of this beautiful web of life.

Einstein said: *Something is moving.* Life is inherently in motion. Action creates vibration. This becomes quite apparent when we use our own voice to awaken our bodies. Whether we call it talking, toning, chanting, shouting or singing, the resonance within us is quite obvious. As we play with all the different tonal qualities of sound, we feel movement within. We feel more alive and connected to ourselves and others around us, including all the plant and animal life. Many native tribes around the world included singing and rhythmic dancing as part of their daily activities.

Imagine your body as a vehicle. Just like an automobile, there is a mechanical way that it works. It needs regular tune-ups, oil, fuel and cleaning. Every individual needs to discover what their body requires to stay tuned up and running smoothly. Singing is a very natural and simple activity to integrate into our routine throughout the day. It's like an internal vibration massage for all the organs.

Taking care of our body temple is one of the most important things we do in our life. When we are healthy, vital, flexible and strong, when all the systems run smoothly, it feels pleasurable to inhabit our own body. We have energy to be, do and have what we need and want. We have enthusiasm to help others and serve our community. Life is joyful and creative.

Awareness Practice

Make a list of all the things you do to take care of your body. (Drink water, sleep, eat, exercise, health practitioner visits, bathing, meditation, etc.) See what kind of flowing pattern you can create to integrate gracefully and harmoniously all these activities into your lifestyle. Find the natural groove of your own body rhythms.

Nature Bath

The Tao is experienced through the freedom that comes from flowing with our internal, natural rhythms. Its essence lies in the natural forces of nature. Its teachings do not involve moral, social or political standards, but simply call for a return to natural simplicity, flowing with nature. Being rather than Trying.

— John Ortiz

Who among us does not love the sight, smell and sound of the ocean while feeling the grains of sand between your toes and tasting the salty air. There is something so elemental about it that dissolves all discord. Maybe it's because our blood is so similar to seawater and we go through daily mood changes like the tides.

When I am near the sea, simple, easy breathing comes naturally and effortlessly. Every thing seems to be in perfect harmony. I feel the power of nature to heal. Perhaps this is because we *are* Nature. Nature *is* us. We are born from and made up of the same material as the forest, the ocean and the animals.

When I feel *out of sorts*, a dose of the natural world provides me with deep refreshment as it awakens the five senses. Tasting the sound of wind and water. Reveling in the touch of the breeze and sun upon my skin. Drinking in the natural colors that rest so easy on the eyes. The feel of dirt under my feet. It's all such comforting music to my soul.

The thing I appreciate most about close contact with nature is tuning into the rhythms and cycles of the elements. The pulse of waves on the shore, the melody of birdsong and the harmony of wind soughing through the pines. How comforting it feels in my own body, listening to this symphony perform its music in such a wide variety of textures and tones. The awareness of how all things work together inspires gratitude in my heart. I am happy to be alive, sharing this planet with all forms of life.

In contrast, the modern world we inhabit can be far removed from these sensations. In our daily lives, we may be more familiar with the sound of machines, the color and smell of roads and buildings.

In the rush of striving for success, raising families, and meeting obligations, it's easy to forget the simple pleasure of quiet time in a natural setting. Yet it is the most basic form of rejuvenation that exists. Our ancestors knew only this, along with the basic instincts of love, fear, and survival. Perhaps we still retain a shard of this primal essence within our being. To be able to awaken and reignite this force is a valuable tool.

My favorite activities for renewal are hiking, kayaking and canoeing. In fact, I wrote this chapter while resting on the beach during a kayak journey in an estuary along the California coast. Whether we paddle or peddle, stretch, walk, swim, dance or run, connection to our animal nature is a crucial component in truly knowing ourselves and our place in the world.

As I sit and contemplate this orchestra of nature around me, I feel at peace. I am content to accept myself just the way I am. All the myriad aspects of my personality harmonize and work together for the good of all. My health improves as I flow with the innate rhythms of this body, my body, the vehicle I have been given to navigate life on this Earth body. Let it be a dance.

Awareness Practice

Take a walk where there are some trees or grass. Maybe you live near the desert or a river, a lake or the ocean. Any form of nature provides a feast for the senses. Listen to the natural elements around you. What kind of music can you distill from the sonic palette that surrounds you? What kind of color combinations do you notice? What does the stillness sound like? What does the air taste like? Can you feel your breath as part of the orchestra? Can you drop into a place of peace for a few moments, no matter what the weather? Can you let yourself be nurtured by the music of nature?

Jimmy Buffet sings: *The sound of the weather is Heavens ragtime band.*

Get It Done

Tao abides in non-action,
yet nothing is left undone.

— Lao Tzu

Have you ever waited until the last minute to complete a project? If you're like me and so many others, the answer is probably yes. Over time and years of experience, I have finally developed my own process of getting things done. I strive for a natural balance between planning things out and allowing things to unfold in their own right timing.

It took three years of consistent attention for me to complete my music CD, *Peace Is Now*. There were 35 musicians involved from around the globe, over 200 tracks of music and more than 250 hours in the recording studio, tracking, mixing and mastering.

Before starting, I worked out a plan with my recording engineer. Then I created a model of the finished product along with charts and diagrams of the steps to follow. I had my map. Once I launched, I stayed the course, month after month, while remaining flexible to incorporate new ideas as the project evolved. It was fascinating to watch myself go through every possible mood swing during the process of creating this piece of music. I experienced moments of elation and perfection alongside doubts of whether the project would ever get finished. Yet somehow I knew that it would. I had done this before and had the confidence that I could do it. But something this large and visionary was akin to leaving the comfortable harbor and sailing out to sea. The far horizon called me toward an unknown land and new forms of creativity.

I have learned that it is vital to let go of perfection in the arts. I have watched many people embark upon the artistic journey and then abandon it before their project was finished. They grew restless or felt they had outgrown that particular expression or artistic concept. But art is timeless. The listener or the observer does not need to know how old it is, how long it took to create or what the artist went through to create it. They simply have an experience of the final product, often in surprising alignment with what the artist put into it.

When you start a project, I encourage you to stay with it until it is done. After it is complete, wrap it up with love and let it go. Release it into the world like a newborn child. It has its own life force to carry it forward.

Alan Watts, the English mystic, shares his wisdom with us. *There is no way, no method, no technique which you or I can use to come into accord with the Tao, the way of nature, because every 'how', every 'method' implies a goal. And we cannot make the Tao a goal any more than we can aim an arrow at itself.*

What I hear Alan saying is that there is no one

way of creating life and art that fits everyone. We each discover our own path, no matter how divergent from *normal* it might appear to be. We all learn from tradition and then let it go when a guiding light awakens within us. Trusting that inner impulse is vital in dropping into the Tao, surrendering to the river that carries us.

Awareness Practice

Whenever you start a new project, create a model as soon as you can. Start with a very simple version and keep upgrading it as you progress. It's literally a tangible type of progress report for your subconscious mind. I find it encouraging to see the fruits of my labor in a hold-in-my-hand visual form. If you're not sure where to start, find a comparable concept and copy it exactly. Then modify it and customize it over time as your vision begins to clarify. It's amazing how helpful this tool can be in order to *get it done.*

Challenges on the Path

The Slow Zone

Slow practice
allows your knowledge
to be integrated with your playing,
allowing thoughts to become feeling.

— *Mildred Portney Chase*

The young musician said to the Master, "I often want to play fast, to practice what I'm working on as quickly as I can. It feels more exciting that way."

The Master replied, "I understand this phenomenon. It's very common for people to use this approach when learning music. While it appears to be productive in the short run there can be complications later on. In the long run, it's easier to speed up then to slow down."

Sometimes people practice so fast, they build mistakes into their muscle memory. Maybe some nuance of tone or phrasing gets overlooked. Then they have to go back and relearn the parts.

If one begins slowly and builds up speed over time, it's easier to focus on the more subtle expression that music can evoke. You might find yourself experiencing a depth of feeling that could be missed with continuous rapid execution.

Try listening to each individual note and how it fits into the puzzle of the whole. Notice how the silent spaces stand out and make their presence known.

Taking it slow is about appreciating the richness of each musical moment. Then, after all, if the piece is best performed allegretto, or quickly, the full range of emotion will be present in the performance.

Being in the Tao of Music means letting each composition inform you what tempo is right. Starting slowly actually gives you more time to discover a broader palette of possibilities.

Guitar legend Les Paul has this to say on the subject. *My chops were not that fast. I just learned more of what was in my mind. I figured out long ago that one note can go a long way if it's the right one, and will probably whip the guy with 20 notes.*

Awareness Practice

Take a simple song or a piece of music and practice it very slowly with a metronome. See how evenly you can play or sing it with a sense of feeling. Then gradually increase the speed with ease, making sure you maintain the full range of expression. After you have mastered a faster tempo, come full circle and play it *Down Tempo*. Notice the nuance of tone and emotions you can express in *The Slow Zone*.

Altered States and Creativity

A Way can be a guide,
but not a fixed path.

— Lao Tzu

A common desire of humans is to seek altered states of consciousness in order to live in harmony with the elements and see beyond what is considered normal. Through the use of plants or other substances, one can feel euphoric and have creative visions. There are also many natural ways to achieve an elevated sense of being.

A friend of mine told me a story about a young musician who came to his house to perform a private concert. The setting was ideal for enjoying acoustic music with undivided attention. My friend offered the young performer, who normally did not drink alcohol, a beer. He said, "Sure, why not?" The evening went spectacularly well, with everyone agreeing it was an unusually special experience. Later that evening, my friend commented on the stellar performance and the young man exclaimed, "It was that beer you gave me. I felt completely uninhibited and free to stretch into places I normally don't go!"

Therein lies the magic and enhancing qualities that the influence of alterants can have upon our creativity. But there is inherently a possible danger. The list of popular substances used by artists throughout history is long and impressive. Most of us have heard the stories about famous artists and musicians, of the turbulent reality, the ecstasy and the agony. Alterants exist in a plethora of forms and are often consumed in social settings.

Art and music cultures are often born through experience with alterants. There are many historical examples and one does not need to search far to learn about them. My interest in this subject lies in the awareness of how everything in our environment influences us. Where and how we choose to live has a tremendous impact on how and what we create. I have always been fascinated by the genesis of art. In search of a deeper knowing and sustainable lifestyle, I have experimented with enhanced states of consciousness. Through partaking of various alterants, I have received many insights and gifts of learning.

In some indigenous cultures Shamans spend years in training, learning the medicinal properties of native plants that are used in a ceremonial manner. During these sacred occasions, insight and healing can come through the medicine people or personal visions that an individual might experience. There are very controlled initiation rites to educate young people about the powers of our natural world. Without guidance, it's easy to misuse and misunderstand these subtle teachings.

Scientists are able to extract a single element from medicinal plants. When you isolate an ingredient from the whole, it becomes a drug, with very different energetic properties from the original source. Often the results of consuming these extractions can be miraculous. But sometimes there are negative side effects that can be quite harmful.

In modern times, through the use of plant and pharmaceutical products, artists often have an *ah-ha* breakthrough moment that unlocks a flow of creative output. The challenge, of course, as we have all witnessed, is the debilitating, addictive cycle that can ensue and destroy the creative potential. This path can be a mixed blessing. If one cannot learn self-control, it becomes the proverbial law of diminishing returns. Over a period of time the results become less productive and artists may feel they cannot catalyze their imagination without their ally.

Many people do learn to manage their use of plant and pharmaceutical medicines in a manner similar to ancient shamanic practices. It usually comes back to the age-old adage of moderation. Most human beings will encounter this phenomenon in every discipline. We have to pay attention and choose carefully what is appropriate for our unique, individual body.

Some kinds of natural stimulation can also be quite euphoric. The runners high, the mountain-climbers edge, the skydivers endorphin rush, etc. Exercise becomes a ritual practice for athletes to maintain their ecstatic state. Some practitioners of these sports can sometimes feel anxious if something interrupts their routine.

All of these experiences potentially open a portal into another universe, a glimpse into a different reality, which offers a new perspective on life. The veil is lifted for a brief moment and we connect to the ancient continuum of creativity. After I discovered this source and understood its nature, Life itself opened up for me. Everything is accessible in each and every moment. I am eternally connected with infinite energy. This understanding has increased my ability to be inspired naturally. I can imagine things in my mind and be confident that I'll receive messages and guidance around how to manifest those ideas I have envisioned.

Awareness Practice

Being creative is natural. Every seeker can tap into Life-Force energy. Through intention, meditation, breath-work, dance, sports training or music practice, one can access the muse. Every individual on the path must discover their own balance, their own source. If you are fortunate, you will forge a lifestyle that is sustainable and healthy. You will be living your own Tao of Music.

If you find yourself drawn to explore the world of alterants, it's best to seek out skilled coaches, experienced teachers and mentors to guide your way. When embarking upon the journey, offer a prayer and learn to respect our ancestors and their cultural traditions. In modern times, substance abuse is a serious problem. The substantial world is what we inhabit and what we're made of. We must learn to navigate our vessel safely and creatively without doing harm to ourselves and others.

Machines Are Everywhere

Before there can be sound, there must be vibration.
Vibration implies movement. Without movement there is
silence. Silence implies stillness. To achieve movement we
must disrupt the stillness. To achieve stillness we must
interrupt movement. To achieve harmony in our lives,
we must achieve a balance between the two.

— *John Ortiz*

Machines are everywhere on planet Earth. Even in the most remote areas, airplanes can be heard flying overhead. In urban settings there are thousands of mechanical and electrical devices all around us. They all hum. Many people today are finding it difficult to adapt to all the new electromagnetic frequencies in our environment.

All machines have a rhythm inside their functioning. A good mechanic can tell what is right and what is wrong by the tones and tempo of the music of the machine. They all vibrate and create patterns that send waves out into the universe. Our ears are incredibly sensitive to the subtle differences between sounds. Wherever I am, I can tune into the notes of airplanes, cars, tractors, computers, etc. What appears at first to be a cacophony of noise, eventually melts into an orchestra of extreme complexity.

As a young man I had a short-term job working at an old time printing press. I was printing names on

Christmas cards. All day long I would change the name block, insert the chosen holiday card and watch the paper fly through the machine. The only way I could manage the boredom was by dancing or singing along with the groove. Even though the other employees considered me a bit strange, I got to know the tempo of that machine. Even to this day I can drift back and feel the clickety-clack of that collection of precise metal parts all working together in harmonious production. I can also feel the relaxation in my bones when the run was over and I could step outside to breathe the air and smell the trees. Perhaps the printing press was also relieved to be done for the day and could rest for the night.

Postscript: With the money I earned from this employment I flew to South America and studied the pan-flute music of the Andes. Even here, in the rural mountains, there were large trucks everywhere, transporting people and goods from village to village. I traveled around, listening to pan-flutes, and spent some time learning how to make them from a local craftsman at a market at the train station. He fell in love with my circular pitch pipe for testing the tuning of instruments I wanted to purchase. I gave it to him just before returning home from my travels. Perhaps other travelers to his town, in search of exotic but western-tuned instruments, benefited from his ownership of this music tool.

Awareness Practice

Whenever you find yourself near a machine or close to a railroad track with a train running by, see if you can feel the rhythm and groove of the metal against metal. How many different polyrhythms and melodies can you discern? How many individual sounds can you count? Do the sounds work together in harmony or do they play against each other and create dissonance?

Remember the feeling of being rocked to sleep on a train or in a car? The hypnotic trance of moving through space and time yet sitting perfectly still. If you listen closely the next time you are traveling, you just might experience the source of the hobo's lullaby.

Am I An Artist or Entertainer?

I see musicians spending a lot of time working on the internal details of what they're doing and far less time working on the ways of positioning it in the world. By "positioning it" I don't only mean thinking of ways of getting it to a record company, but thinking of where it could go, where it fits in the cultural picture and what else does it relate to?

— *Brian Eno*

Creativity gushes forth from me in abundance. Every word is a creation, often preceded by a thought, sometimes not! I like being funny, maybe because I like the attention. Or perhaps because it's so fun to see everyone happy and laughing for a moment. Then I'm an entertainer. But I tend to rebel against being entertaining on demand. I prefer to express whatever cultural or spiritual insight I am relishing in the present time. Some might consider this selfish and narcissistic. It's just my style.

I love movies. I love the stories, the colors and the music soundtracks. I don't like every movie I see. Some just don't resonate with me. This is probably true for most people. Yet overall I think the world of film has a tremendous impact on human culture. The tales are born from life experience and in turn, affect the viewers, often in profound ways.

In the milieu of motion pictures, entertainment is often the doorway to some kind of message. The same message can be delivered in many different ways. If it's important, should it be delivered in a serious manner or in a comedy?

There's obviously no correct answer to this question. I have seen both approaches be effective. Some of the most brilliant insights into difficult social issues that I have received have come through comedians. Sometimes you just have to laugh and let go.

But why do I even question this? Filmmaker Alfred Hitchcock pondered the same question. The more famous he became, the more it haunted him. I think most serious artists want to be taken seriously. Perhaps every writer and performer is both, artist and entertainer. And maybe I just enjoy the philosophical discussion and play of words.

In some ways it comes back to the age-old rift between classical and pop culture. Complex art forms verses simple and more accessible genres. There are strong advocates on both sides of the fence. In the end, it always comes back to personal preferences. One persons' garbage is another's treasure.

In the Tao of Music we can flow in either direction, always the path of least resistance. All water ends up in the sea eventually. One day we are freshwater, the next we are full of salt. Stay open to what serves the highest vision and your art will find its perfect place.

Awareness Practice

Ask yourself, "What am I creating and for whom?" "What conversation am I joining?" Whatever our field of interest or expertise, it's a joy to find like-minded souls to connect with. It's also important to learn from another point of view. It always comes back to balance. We need support in developing our art, craft or skill. Then we must test it against the reality of this world. Is what I'm doing valuable to another? We are asking not from a place of doubt, but from authentic inquiry. Spend some part of your creative time playing with these questions and you will discover where and when to make your offering.

One With
the Path

Being Music

Music is the most primordial phenomenon because it is in nature, in the breeze passing through the trees, in the birds singing. You will never find a bird being a philosopher but all birds are musicians. Go and search. You will not find a stream religious, but all streams are musical. Go and ask these winds passing through the trees. They may not have ever heard about the Bible, the Koran or the Bhagavad Gita, but they know music. Music is life itself.

— Osho

Tao of Music is about living in a musical way, choosing to recognize that every sound we hear and every sound we make is a note in the great symphony of life. If we approach our path with beginner's mind and listen carefully to the complex interplay of the different melodies, our contribution will synchronize in perfect rhythm with the larger picture, the whole of life.

Whether we study the art and science of music, or simply appreciate our humble place in the grand orchestra, we all contribute to the creation of this tapestry of harmony and beauty.

Being in the Tao is about taking every step consciously. Whether you are working, resting, playing, daydreaming or visualizing, you know that is what you are doing. Obstacles will surely appear along the path. You can choose to respond creatively to every event and learn from it. Improvise on the themes and melodies that come to you in the flow of life. Find the blessing in every offering.

Everything we do, from cleaning the floor, cooking a meal, or getting a drink of water becomes the Tao. The Way is in being present to whatever is happening now. This presence will translate across the lines of every activity you participate in. Your life composition will gracefully unfold and blossom more beautifully with each moment that you are alive.

I believe this awareness is one of the secrets to a joyful existence here on earth. We are all beginners on the journey that appears before us with each new dawn.

Awareness Practice

With each inhalation, notice what you are doing. Ask yourself, "Where is my attention now?" Feel the rhythm of this activity and how you harmonize the experience with your breath. Over and over again we wake up, however briefly, with love and passion for life. Enjoy the music of the moment. You might find, more often than not, a smile in your heart and a skip in your step.

Where Did That Note Come From?

In the old days our people had no education.
All their wisdom and knowledge came to them from dreams.
They tested their dreams
and in that way learned their own strength.

— *Ojibwa Elder*

The mysterious source of sound, where does it begin? Does it have a start and a finish? We humans seem to have a desire to break things down into small segments, something we can wrap our consciousness around, like a three minute song with a simple but profound message. Then on the other hand, a Wagnerian opera bursts forth from a brilliant mind that can embrace a bigger container.

Creativity springs forth from somewhere and everywhere. Like *The Force*, it is omnipresent. We all access it differently, in our own unique way. To catalog the vast variety of creation that is born every minute of every day would be impossible. The beauty of this awareness is that we don't have to. In the whole of our creative life, we may never know exactly where it comes from. But it's always there. We have only to stop and drink from the pool or just run our fingers through as we dance by, poetry in motion. It doesn't even matter how much we create, it's just so much fun to participate in the flow. It feels so natural to sing, write, dance, draw, play with color and form. This book is focused on music and the sonic world, but all art sources from the same river of vibrations, light, color and sound.

So when you are looking for the next note, it isn't very far away. In fact, it's usually pretty close. Maybe we have to move some energy to clear the debris around it. Perhaps we need to become still, and let the dust settle to reveal the next note. It might even come to us in a dream.

I once was awakened at about five in the morning with the chorus of a song in two part harmony flowing through my mind. It was like two angels singing. In a trance-like state, I sang the melody into my recorder. When I arose, I wrote it down, then spent the next three days walking around the hills to find the verses. Appropriately it is called, *I Will Come For You At Dawn.*

Whether or not we know where the next note will come from, we can always find it somehow, somewhere. Then when it arrives, there is often another note right behind it. And maybe even a whole symphony is revealed in a bright vision, clear as the night sky after a big storm has passed through.

Awareness Practice

Notice all the different melodies that circulate through your brain. Maybe you have a tune that's been with you for a while. One that appeared some time ago and you find yourself humming it. Chances are it's a blend of different songs that you have heard over the years. See if you can track it down, remember it, and make it your own motif.

Most art is a re-mix of ideas that have gained new relevance or meaning. Every generation expresses itself in the current language or style of the times. World mantra singers Deva Premal and Miten say it beautifully:

Keep your heart strong and sing your own song.

Cricket Therapy

Never mistake a rut for a deep groove.

— Richie Hayward

In the cool of a summer evening, the most healing sound emanates from the forest; Crickets. Just hearing their name brings a calm to my nerves. Hypnotic polyrhythms gently reach into my soul as each individual sound tentacle dances its way into my heart.

I can't help but close my eyes and breathe it in. The vibration, the pulse as it undulates so smooth, then... jumps a beat, like the snare drum in pop music on the *One-AND* instead of the typical back-beat on *One-TWO*. (In music language, that's one-half of a beat earlier). It keeps me in the trance but accents and highlights a different reality for a moment. Then, before I know it, the chorus lifts me up and gently lays me back into a steady rhythm. And the *Holy Grail of Groove* is bestowed upon me.

From another perspective, for some folks the sound of crickets could be quite irritating. The high pitched oscillations might actually be painful to a very sensitive ear. As always, in the Tao of Music, the journey of each of us is to discover the sounds that resonate with our core, that inspire us to live our passion in life. Find the songs of the animal world that feel good to you and drop into the sacred space that is created between the listener and the sound. Maybe it's a birdsong, an elephant call or the cicadas in the summertime. When you tune into a resonant frequency and allow it to expand your senses, a healing calm can blossom in your being.

Wikipedia says: *Crickets are mainly nocturnal, and are best known for the loud, persistent, chirping song of males trying to attract females, although some species are mute. The singing species have good hearing via the tympani (eardrums) on the tibiae of the front legs.*

It's fascinating to me how much of the music of nature is created for a very practical purpose. Yet when we listen, we are able to abstract from it whatever beauty and meaning we can imagine.

This kind of listening experience has been very therapeutic for me. It's a natural healing modality. When we listen closely to our inner and outer world, our body-mind knows exactly what we need. I'm not advocating the replacement of personal growth work, just looking to expand the territory.

Awareness Practice

Spend some time listening to the sounds of animals and birds. Frogs singing together is one of my favorites. The purring of your cat has an amazing groove to it. The polyrhythmic play of a neighborhood full of dogs might be more interesting if you concentrate on the call and response of all the players. And the coyotes, what a horn section!

As you listen with awareness to the animal kingdom, allow a comforting sense of *belonging* on this planet to germinate in your soul.

Peace and Reconciliation

Music is a tool to create healing and activate people to change things. Music promotes the bridging of all tribes. When it is real, raw and honest storytelling about what you've been through, people connect with it. I think that's the most important thing you can do with music.

— Nahko Bear

My father, Edward Stephen John Setchko (1926–2009), was one of my biggest fans and supporters. He loved music. He played the drums in his high school jazz band in New York. Once he told me a story about how he sat in for a tune with the Tommy Dorsey Band when they passed through his town in the early 1940's.

He joined the US Navy when he was seventeen and became the captain of a small troop carrier ship in the South Pacific. When he came back from the war, he earned a degree in psychology and then went on to become a minister. When I was young I remember him being a consultant to churches around the country. His last job before retiring was as a professor of theology. He was always supporting causes he believed in and frequently donated money to local musicians to help them with their work.

Toward the end of his career, Ed started the *Project for Peace and Reconciliation in the Middle East.* His mission and purpose was to facilitate peaceful interactions between Israelis and Palestinians. He would travel to Israel for a month or two every year and told me stories about clandestine meetings in secret houses. He and his colleagues would share ideas for peace and take turns doing hands-on healing work.

My dad took some of my cassettes with him when he traveled and sometimes my flute would be playing in the background during the sessions. He said the music would help create the sacred space they needed to feel safe doing this work. I am grateful that he was able to integrate our paths in this precious way.

In a similar way, some of my music has been used in spas, chiropractic offices and yoga studios around the world. It establishes a healing tone in the environment and creates an ambience of peace. I have also received letters from a few mothers who listened to the music during labor. After the birth, they would often use the same music to calm and soothe their child.

These are some examples of how music can be used to enhance environments and assist in healing and transformation. It's quite magical how powerful music can be. In some ways, my *Peace Is Now* project is a blossoming of a seed my father planted in me as a youth. I am forever grateful for the inspiration of his work in the world. David Byrne of the *Talking Heads* wisely said: *Far from being merely entertainment, music, I would argue, is a part of what makes us human.*

Awareness Practice

As an experiment sometime, try using music more consciously than just putting it on as background soundpaper. Create a beautiful setting and put some music on that helps you invoke sacred space. Perhaps you'll feel moved to dance, sing or hum along. Or maybe just drop into the stillness of the moment and let any cares or concerns fade away. If you want to connect deeply with another person or a pet, invite them to join you. Make it a weekly ritual and use the time to come back to your center. Take a deep breath and relax with a sigh. Peace is now.

If you are a composer of music, a creator of art or a business person with a mission and a purpose, try infusing your work with positive intentions for the world. Subliminal communication is a powerful agent for change.

Letting Go
Of the Path

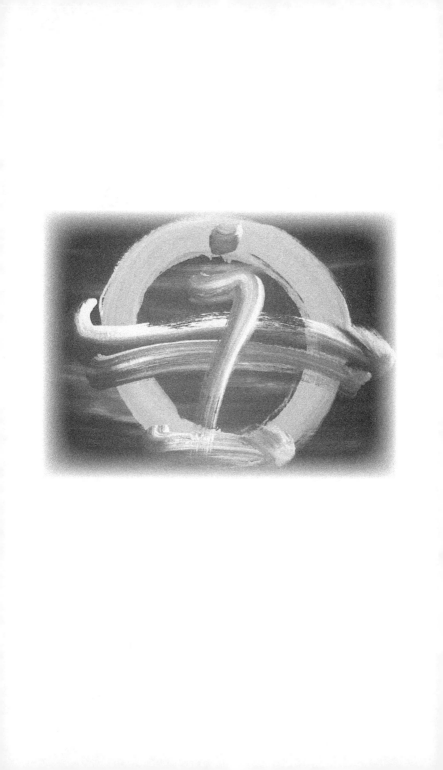

Dancing To Your Own Melody

If a person hears the Tao in the morning
and dies in the evening, his life
has not been wasted.

— Chuang Tzu

Every morning I awake and give thanks to be alive. I start listening to the music in my head and imagine the best possible outcome for all the activities of my day. So many different melodies cascading through my brain. Which one will I choose? The timbre of my parents concerned voices? The groove of government verbiage? The libretto of tasks to be done by noon? The tones of educational institutions? The sweet strains of religion?

After listening to this cacophony, I take a deep breath and relax into the clear rhythms of my own heart and the pure sonorities of my own voice. The voice that believes in me and is composed of my highest dreams and visions. It is such a refreshing tonic for my soul. This is the source I want to consult for the ultimate word on which direction the song of my life is headed. When all is said and done, there's nothing quite like dancing to your own melody.

Awareness Practice

Every morning when you wake up, take a few moments to breathe and pay attention to all the voices arising in your consciousness. Notice how each thought makes you feel in your body. Choose the words and ideas that support your well-being and create a feeling of excitement to be alive. Keep a pen and paper or some kind of recorder by the bedside and capture these precious morning gifts. There might be something creative and exciting that bubbles up and will float away forever unless you remember it. You never know when the great choreographer will call you into the dance.

Free Fall

Leave your stepping stones behind,
something calls for you.
– Bob Dylan

There is always something new. I learn from the past, honor it, and let go. Visions call to me from some deep well. I'm never quite sure where I will end up. Having some kind of container to drop my ideas into can be helpful, like concrete and ice need a form to take shape.

Music often entices me into a creative zone. The sound of voices and instruments dancing together in rhythm and harmony. I pour myself into well used genres and time tested traditions, then expand into new territory. If I'm lucky, some gift reveals itself and I feel the ecstasy of creation. When I share it, and another being appreciates it, the joy is doubled.

Maybe only Mother Nature hears my song. The wind, coyotes, a bird, a kitten or a bobcat. Perhaps the ocean will receive my creation and throw back some applause in the spray that moistens the air.

What is beckoning to me? Dare I try to label it? Will I ever catch a glimpse of the muse that so insistently dances into my waking world and my dream life? The call is so mythic, iconic and primordial. There are new horizons, unknown territories, and fresh beginnings. Is redemption on the other side? Can I open to something greater in myself and discover peace in my heart? I suppose the impulse to leave the familiar stepping stones is a gift in itself. I am grateful just to feel the tickle of creativity in my soul.

Benjamin Hoff says this in the *Tao Of Pooh*: *And what is Taoism? It's really very simple. It calls for living without preconceived ideas about how life should be lived. But it's not a preconception of how life... It's... Well, you'd do better to listen to Pooh, if you really want to find out.*

Awareness Practice

Once a week, do something completely out of the ordinary. Something that is unusual for you. Walk to a familiar destination by a different route. Call somebody you have not spoken to in a year. Open to a random page in a magazine or book that is completely outside of your usual subject matter and read a few paragraphs. Experiment with that new health food you've been hearing about. Pick up a musical instrument that you've never played and make some sounds. Keep tossing the dice and find things that amuse and inspire you. Make a new friend. Run in the rain without an umbrella. Listen to what is calling you.

Relax In The Quilence

Deep Silence.
I love that sound track more than any other.
It is the source of all sound which is beyond manifestation.

— *Steve Bollock*

When a nine year old boy comes to you and says he made up a new word, it's best to pay attention. I was relaxing in the local coffee shop, reading my book in progress. A man stood by me, waiting in line to use the restroom. I could tell he might be there for a bit so I offered him my book to entertain himself.

As he was reading, his son bounced up and asked if I wanted to hear the new word he made up. I said, "Yes, of course!" He said, "Quilence, the quiet in the silence." I was stunned. All my life I have been dancing between these two words, seeking a bridge that crosses the gap and spans the chasm! I asked him, "Can I use that word in my new book?" He said, "Sure," and ran off before I could engage him further. His Dad and I just acknowledged each other with that familiar look of, "Out of the mouths of babes..."

Throughout my music career I have often thought about this zone between quiet and silence. How much of the sound spectrum can humans perceive? I know we can hear very loud noises and at a certain amplitude or volume, the sonic waves can destroy our hearing mechanism. But can we experience total silence? Sometimes we can *feel* a low frequency wave in our body, but not *hear* it with our ears. There is a dog whistle that humans can't hear but our pets can. I've heard that scientists can create a vacuum where there is no sound. Yet even in that environment, I think we could hear a soft humming in our ears, the internal vibration of our own body.

Now when I'm listening to the sounds of life around me, and it's not totally silent but definitely in the lower threshold of quiet, I can relax in the quilence.

Awareness Practice

Some definitions to consider:

Sound: The movement of air waves that bounce off our ear drums. A frequency that is audible to the human ear.

Silence: A near impossible experience of no sound, or total absence of sound, complete stillness.

Quiet: A relatively low threshold of sound, little or no noise. Hushed, soft or muted sounds.

How does your own experience compare to these definitions? If an air wave is below or above our perception range, is it still sound? It's quite likely there will be as many interpretations of these words as there are people. The existential question might arise, "If no one hears the sound wave, does it exist?"

Silence

The artist must say it without saying it.

— Duke Ellington

Epilogue
Gratitude For The Path

What a gift it has been to be on this path. So many wonders and delights, along with a multitude of challenges. Every journey has a few rough spots along the way. There is so much to learn, so many surprises, curve balls, and unexpected choices to make.

I practice being in the Tao, going with the flow, like water, letting go, again and again. At some mystical point in time, without explanation or hyperbole, it all makes sense. There is simply a quiet knowing of being in the right place, doing the right thing, creating what needs to be expressed in this now moment.

So many beautiful souls have held up a light for me, created sacred containers and guided me through many storms. I hope this book can be a part of your journey in some small way. I am grateful for you joining me in the conversation.

Acknowledgments

All of these amazing people supported, laughed or played music with me, and generally inspired me to stay creative and finish this book.

Amanda Kreglow, Art Hills, Barbara Juniper, Diane Poslosky, Jim Cody, Jennifer Mann, Joyus Lippincott, Karyl Huntley, Kaz Tanahashi, Linda Kazynski, Mary Murray Shelton, Patrick Woodworth, Robert Adamich, Robert Powell, Robin Zickel, Stephen Meese, Steve Bollock and Tarangita.

A special thanks to my editor, Francine Huss, who encouraged me to clarify my ideas and smooth out the rough edges of the manuscript.

Inspirational Resources

Favorite Books

Creative Mind And Success	Ernest Holmes
Creativity for Life	Eric Maisel
How Music Works	David Byrne
Just Being At The Piano	Mildred P. Chase
Music	Sufi Inayat Khan
Music As Yoga	Patrick Bernard
One Square Inch Of Silence	Gordon Hampton
	John Grossman
Practicing The Presence	Joel Goldsmith
Tao Te Ching	Lao Tzu
Tao, The Watercourse Way	Alan Watts
The Great Animal Orchestra	Bernie Krause
The Listening Book	W. A. Mathieu
The Mindful Hiker	Stephen Altschüler
The Music Lesson	Victor L. Wooten
The Tao Of Pooh	Benjamin Hoff
The Tao Of Willie	Willie Nelson
The Yoga of Sound	Russill Paul
The Way Of Chuang Tzu	Thomas Merton
To Live As We Are	Sachiko Adachi
Zen Guitar	Philip Toshio Sudo

Other Works by Bodhi

Books

Body Is Sky	Poetry And Photos
Spirit	Original Chants
The World Is My Ashram	Poetry

Instrumental Music CD's

Cafe Tropique	with Crystal Wind
Cloud Etchings	Tibetan Bowls & Flute
Harbin Temple	Flute Concert
Inner Traveler	with Crystal Wind
Ocean Whispers	Flute & Ocean Duet
Shamanic Flute	Solo Flute
Trans Ukraine	Flutronica
Qi	Flute Meditations

Vocal Music CD's

Born To Sing	Debut Album
LIVE 5.16.09	Bodhi & Friends
Peace Is Now	with 35 musicians
Spirit	Original Chants
Tonight	with Stephen Meese

Poetry & Music CD's

Humans Are Slow Fires	with Patrick Woodworth
Winds Of Dawn	with Steve Ryals

About Bodhi
Living Life As Music

Bodhi Setchko is a musician, author, songwriter, composer, recording artist, producer, teacher, band leader, sound healer, poet, speaker, workshop leader and creativity coach. The founder of recording/touring ensembles, *CRYSTAL WIND* and *RHYTHM MATRIX*, he has recorded 14 albums of original music. He has been performing and providing concert quality music for special events, weddings, workshops and church services for over 30 years. As of 2016, he has been the music director for eleven years at the "Golden Gate Center for Spiritual Living" in Northern California, with Rev. Karyl Huntley.

Having studied with many fine musicians, including renowned artists Paul Horn, William Mathieu, and G. S. Sachdev, he developed a unique style of improvisation and composition using the sounds of nature as his inspirational source. He has also contributed his flute tones to the recordings of many contemporary musicians.

As a master of the flute, piano, guitar, conch shell or turning an affirmation into a chant, Bodhi brings a genuine lightness of being to every concert and workshop setting. His music empowers people to manifest their deepest dreams and desires. His CD, *TRANS UKRAINE* was #1 Ambient Album of the year in 2006. You can hear the flute music of *BODHI (New Age)*, on Pandora Internet Radio and numerous other streaming sites.

Bodhi is available for teaching, concerts, church services, workshops, speaking engagements, coaching sessions, and Tao of Music seminars.

ksetchko@yahoo.com

twitter: @bodhistar

bodhisetchko.com

shamanicflute.com

CPSIA information can be obtained
at www.ICGtesting.com
Printed in the USA
LVHW091342180219
607890LV00001B/2/P